Secrets of Runes for Wicca Beginners

Start to learn how to Use Runes if you are an absolute wicca Beginner. How to become a Witch with the Ancient Knowledge of Viking Runes.

Laura Hatwood

© Copyright 2024 Laura Hatwood - All rights reserved.

The content contained within this book may not be reproduced, duplicated or transmitted without direct written permission from the author or the publisher.

Under no circumstances will any blame or legal responsibility be held against the publisher, or author, for any damages, reparation, or monetary loss due to the information contained within this book. Either directly or indirectly.

Legal Notice:

This book is copyright protected. This book is only for personal use. You cannot amend, distribute, sell, use, quote or paraphrase any part, or the content within this book, without the consent of the author or publisher.

Disclaimer Notice:

Please note the information contained within this document is for educational and entertainment purposes only. All effort has been executed to present accurate, up to date, and reliable, complete information. No warranties of any kind are declared or implied. Readers acknowledge that the author is not engaging in the rendering of legal, financial, medical or professional advice. The content within this book has been derived from various sources. Please consult a licensed professional before attempting any techniques outlined in this book.

By reading this document, the reader agrees that under no circumstances is the author responsible for any losses, direct or indirect, which are incurred as a result of the use of information contained within this document, including, but not limited to, errors, omissions, or inaccuracies.

Table of Contents

Introduction 7

Chapter 1 15

The Importance of Runes in Magic

Chapter 2 26

Magic and Runes

Chapter 3 33

The Study of Runes

Chapter 4 37

Runes Divination

Chapter 5 41

How to Read Runes

Chapter 6 54

Runes Tips

Chapter 7 58

The 13 Steps to Achieve the Runes Power

Chapter 8 63

The Ancient Advice of Rune Readings

Chapter 9 67

The Runes Popularity

Chapter 10 74

Rune Crystals

Chapter 11 79

The Way Psychics Use Runes

Chapter 12 84

How to Use Runes to Survive

Chapter 13 91

Psychic Runes

Chapter 14 .... **98**

Rune Symbols

Chapter 15 .... **105**

Using Runes for Divination

Chapter 16 .... **109**

What Could Norse Mythology Teach You About Runes?

Chapter 17 .... **126**

The Origin and Purpose Behind the Ancient Symbols and Alphabet

Chapter 18 .... **135**

Secret Of Using Runes During The Correct Month For Rune Magic

Chapter 19 .... **139**

Viking Rune Casting Tips and Information

Chapter 20 .... **149**

Building the Rune Sorcery Ritual

Introduction

Runes were originally used in a number of ancient alphabets dating back to the year 150AD, which was originally used by the East Goths, and then adopted in other parts of Europe and Scandinavia. Although they were commonly used primarily as a form of communication for hundreds of years, they were eventually replaced by the Latin alphabets. Despite the fact that these symptoms were eventually replaced in everyday use, the use of runes is completely missing. Runes are still associated with mythology or perhaps used for decorative purposes, especially in the Scandinavian countries.

In addition, it is used for practical linguistic purposes, the runes were also used for magic, and the Diviner's purpose, with the tradition of casting the runes and the runes reading, is almost as old as language itself.

It is not surprising that the word rune itself comes from the Anglo- Saxon word meaning "secret" and still carries a very mystical air.

Reading traditionally begins with the fact that the subject asks for runes. The tiles are then placed in a closed bag, and randomly pick up the motif, or thrown on a flat surface, randomly before reading them. Then they can be read separately or combined in what is known as promotion. You can create different templates or expanded depending on the questions that were asked in the session. Some readers will have more tilesets, with each set associated with a different question or theme, such as love or friendship.

Tiles could be set on clay, stone, glass, resin, or polished pebbles if the pebbles used were often collected in person from the site, which has considerable mystical significance or has a huge personal meaning for the reader. These pebbles will then be marked or engraved during a mystical ritual using a special boat.

This is traditional; at the end of the ritual, the destruction of the stick is to prevent its use for any other purpose, because it can cause neutrality challenge tiles. Although many books have been issued to explain the phenomenon of reading the runes, and also how it is not uncommon for each reader on their system.

Although it is traditional for the subject to be physically present during reading, in some cases, it is possible to do reading on the phone or over the internet. In such cases, reading will have a slightly different format, but the result of reading should not be affected if the reader is a qualified specialist.

Well, runes are a lot of things. For example, they are an ancient Nordic Alphabet. And they are also magical symbols. They are not widely known among modern people, but they are still used, not as an alphabet anymore, but allocates used for divination and magical purposes. Keep reading, and you will learn everything you need to know about runes as a beginner.

Runes are also known as Elder Futhark - this is the Nordic runic alphabet, consisting of 24 runes. The runes themselves are symbols, written or carved on stone or wood, or even paper. They are believed to be a gift from Odin, the Nordic god, and it has the magical power to attract love, money, friendship, and success. The word "rune" itself means "secret" or "whisper," and this makes the runes magical symbols very mysterious for that same day.

From a scientific point of view, it is difficult to learn the age of runes. Some researches tend to believe that they have existed for more than 3 thousand years. Most scientists agree that they are not more than 2 thousand years old. From the mythological point of view, the runes are the gift of Odin, who was hung on the tree of life for nine days and nights, and was blessed with the wisdom of the runes. Later, he passed on his knowledge to humans.

Runes were used mainly as a magic Alphabet. They were used for divination and prediction of the future. They were also used to sculpt whole sentences called "runic formulas or runic scripts." Such formulas were aimed at attracting wealth and success by magical means. Runes have also been used to make talismans and amulets called "bindrunes." A bindrune is a symbol made of two or three different runes connected to each other, and it is a very powerful magic talisman.

In the old days, runes were used by northerners, Vikings, and inhabitants of the British Isles. Northern Europe was also not without runes. They were used by druids for magical rituals, winning victory in battle, attracting a good harvest, etc. still today runes are used. However, no one writes more about it. The Elder Futhark symbols are still used for divination and the creation of talismans. You can find many books on the topic, and even the Guild of modern Druids who still use runes. You can also learn runic magic for your own purpose; if you want, there are many resources out there.

With runes, you can attract good work, love, and friendship, business success, material and spiritual wealth, health, and many other things. If you're looking for a peaceful but mysterious magic system, the runes will be the best to start with.

Chapter 1

What Is Rune Magic?

Magic Rune Symbols

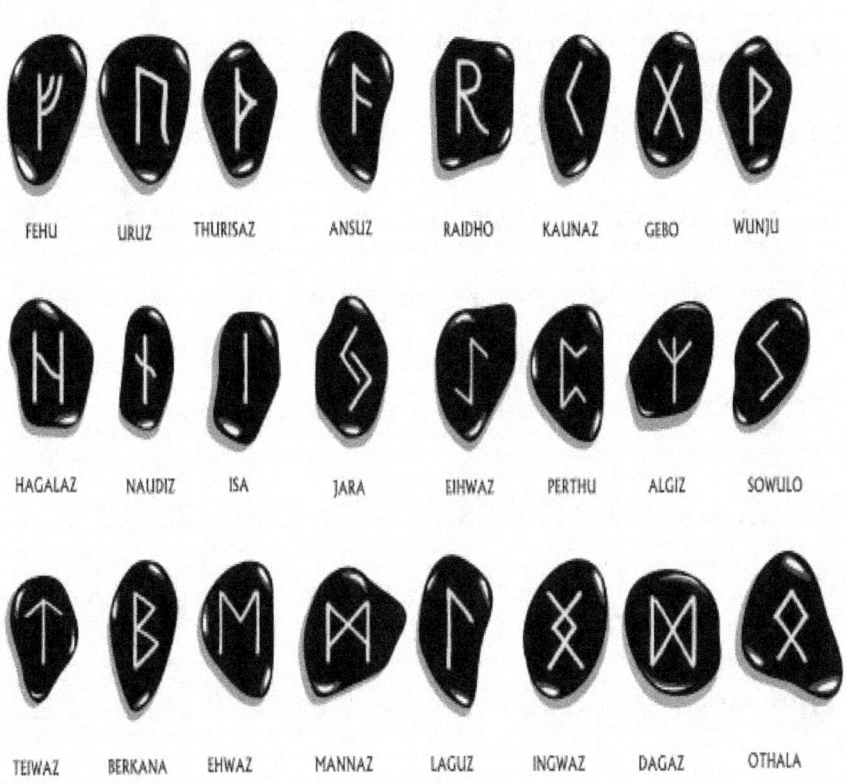

I tried to share with you the importance of placing runes and gods/goddesses of the North until the 21st century.

We shouldn't rune in to the forest with axes and swords, drinking mead (if we don't want to talk), pray to the gods/goddess to help us; if we had the power to invoke Odin, Thor or Tyr in our stain, or our rituals. What would we do with them?

We can't get them out of the outside world.

We must attract Odin's wisdom, thor's strength, and Tyr's courage. IN OUR LIVES, IN OUR AURAS.

Then we'll be Odin, Thor, and Tyr 21st century. This is the age to do it yourself.

Runes, Odin, gods/goddesses, and the North belong to the 21st century The Age of Aquarius, The Age of the Internet, and quantum physics.

We can't ask them to do it for us anymore. We have to ask ourselves how to do it and put energy on it.

It is incorrect to keep runes tied to the Viking Age.

Parables, paradoxes, and puzzles overshadow all the literature about the magic of runes.

The laws of quantum physics penetrated the mystery of the magic of rune symbols.

Runes were never meant for prophecy.

Runes should never have been used as an alphabet.

Runes are universal creative energy. Magic rune symbols are just Magical symbols that connect us with the runic energy of the quantum Ocean (the spirit of God).

True Rune Symbols

Here are some definitions of runic symbols, which will share with you the reasons why runic symbols are powerful and magical.

The rune Symbol is the body that contains the soul. (rune contour body containing the soul of living Runic energies).

A rune symbol is the matter holding meaning. (Rune outline plus rune meaning).

A rune symbol is a focus of strength. (each rune symbol embodies different Rune energies).

Rune symbol is a capacitor of consciousness. (It takes a piece of quantum consciousness of the ocean (the spirit of god) and condenses it into a rune form).

A rune symbol is a reservoir of thought. (by meditating on the rune, you can extract useful Rune thoughts from the quantum Ocean (the spirit of god).

Magic rune symbols are energy exchanges between very different levels, worlds, and intelligent beings operating through them, you and the World Rune.)

It is Rune Energy, Rune meanings, Rune associations, and life force enclosed in any rune symbol that is alive and functional for you. Odin just rediscovered the runes. They extend beyond the Viking Age.

To be a Rune Master, you must constantly feed your inner being to be deeper with higher levels of frequencies from the rune energy level.

Look for runes or die!

Let's look at some definitions of Rune Magic.

Magic runes reduce laws higher than current ones.

Rune magic causes remote action without having to use a physical object.

Rune Magic uses the law of resonance frequencies and life force.

Magic Runeallows vital power to circulate between similar and identical subjects.

Rune Magic is the ability to allow running energies that flow from the quantum ocean (god's spirit) into your body and life.

Magic rune smashes chains of poverty, liberation from slavery diseases, ending misery failure.

To succeed in the magic of rune, you need three operational forces. Rune Energy - - - A Rune Symbol Lens - - - Your Photos

Life force --- the power of your mind.

Sitting on a chair and meditating, looking at the magical symbol of the rune you create.

Living Runic Thought Form.

Your mind has provided the power to combine the rune symbol in your hands, and the rune energy in the quantum ocean, bring them into your body and life.

There are three ingredients you need to perform magic rune. Runic energies that are specific frequencies in the quantum ocean

This new form of Runic thinking will now be a part of your energy field.

This form of Runic thinking will make a cyber ally strive and achieve its goals.

Rune Uruz (health) example:

If it is uruz energy rune that you have attracted to your aura, this form of Rune thinking will look for the cause of poor health in your body. This will then attract people, places, and events you need to take care of yourself.

Every time you use rune magic to fulfill your desires, the universe decides the details of how to achieve it.

While all this is happening outside of you, the Uruz rune energy in your aura dissolves the energy blocks that caused your illness.

You need to be open and aware of new thoughts, people, feelings, and places caused by the rune form of thinking.

Magic Runeallows you to develop your spiritual and psychic abilities.

With your ability to attract rune energy, you can attract health, wealth, and love to your life now.

Remember, runes are energy. These are universal creative energies.

Runes are housed in an endless quantum Ocean (the spirit of god), where time does not exist. There is no past, present, or future; Just time.

Thousands of years ago, Father Odin was suspended for nine days and nights in the Yggdrasil tree. He finally reached the quantum Ocean (the spirit of god) and rediscovered the runes for us.

Christianity constantly tried to erase all information about runes.

Guido von List, the German rune Master, had cataract surgery in the twentieth century. Lying in his blind bed, he also reached the quantum Ocean (the spirit of god) and discovered the runes again.

This page is about the runes, and the Runes of energy with practical information that you can use to attract health, wealth, and love into your life now.

The magic rune uses runes as keys to the universal energy of creation. Runes were used for spiritual purposes, long before anyone started writing.

Rune Magic will help you get in touch with worlds and energy far beyond your daily life.

Runes are the energies that preceded the language.

This page gives you some reasons for how Rune Magic works.

I have many pages about Rune meditations, Rune Yoga, rune rituals, etc. which will show that now, you have to attract runes into your life.

The magic rune is very powerful, and you can use it to attract health, wealth, and love.

Chapter 2

Runes in Magic

The runes were discovered on objects made of wood, stone, metal, and bones. Wood is the most preferred way to Represent breeds, especially for magical functions. The words for "pieces of wood" associated with runes are different in the old tradition.

Three ancient Scandinavian examples related to runes would be stafr (stave, letter, and secret tradition), tenin (twig, talismanic word for divination), and hlutr (a lot for divination, a talismanic object on which the runes were carved).

On the bracts (thin metal discs encoded runes and various other patterns) play an important role in magical use. Among the ways in which runes were used in magic is that the additional concealment of a magic formula with complex codes formulated. These codes were created to keep runic magic messages secret.

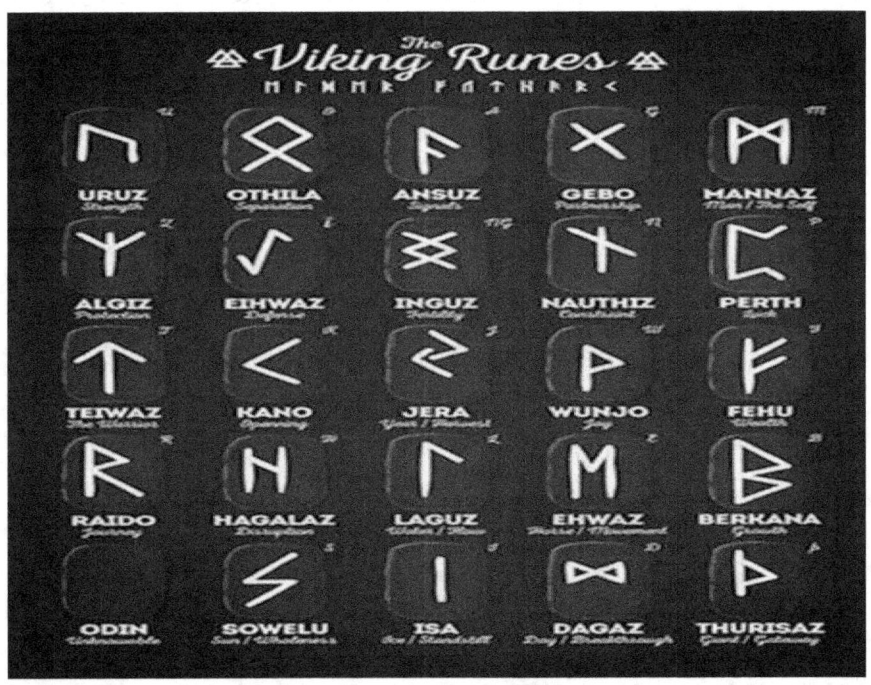

The cornerstone of all rune codes is the numerical value of runes. The two younger and older futharks are divided into three groups called aettir (families). The futharks of the runes are a mystery for the systems that have been developed mainly in the Futhark younger of the time; however, they were certainly known and used in the next period, since ancient representations of the old row are also clearly divided into aettir.

The names of tent branches and runes know the two most remarkable techniques of creating secret rune codes. Runes can be used magically widely. The most basic technique of runic magic in ancient times was talismanic, that is, the runes are carved into many of the objects, and infused by psychic power for a change in the vitki (Master of the runes) or its surroundings.

Runes are especially useful in magical works related to triumph, success, protection, and salvation from restrictions, love, and the acquisition of wisdom.

Each rune has a name that was also a meaningful word. It is reliable that the names of the runes have survived since the earliest times, although, of course, they are not recorded until late, when the written records of the script began.

The names of the Norwegian runes are preserved a little later, and at a time when only sixteen letters survived in Scandinavia, so we do not have a complete list of the names of this region. Usually, the names of the runes began with the sound represented by the rune.

Divination is another important use of Viking races. The forms of the runes were often carved from pieces of wood, poured on white fabric, made a reading of the runes. While it was read according to strict criteria, all methods are valid today and very effective for magical purposes. Runes are sacred signs that can be used as focal points for the defense of magic, meditation, self-transmutation, and mysterious communication.

Runic divination is one of the oldest prophetic systems in Northern Europe. The runes form a powerful key that offers the main course of the inner secrets of Northern Europe. Using runes, we restore contacts within the plan and recover most of our lost knowledge.

For true divination, the communication channel must be performed by runes. They should be accepted to speak for themselves without disturbing the analytical mind.

Divination is the origin of the Blessed act of obtaining advice from the gods. The power of magical control, and the dark side of consciousness, part of which is divination, is in the North-European sense of Odin.

These forces represent the past, the present, and the future and distinguish three goddesses or barrels, Urs, Verdandi, and Skult- weaving a network of Destiny, Destiny, or orlog.

Therefore, the runes are sacred and intimately related to Nordic mythology, personifying our deepest spiritual values. To find the maximum benefit of runes, it is necessary to have basic knowledge and understanding of Northern myths, and various divine forms and archetypes. This is what divination was supposed to be and how it was used in ancient times.

Chapter 3

Learn How to Study Runes from the Beginning

Make. Make. Make. Who am I? How is it used?

Runes exist from time immemorial. In recent history (since 2000 years), they have appeared three times in human affairs. The first time was about 1000 years ago when the Vikings ruled the world. They carried them on their dragon ships, leaving their traces on stones and monuments around the world.

At the end of the twentieth century, they again ascended to Germany, and Guido von List and other German Mystics again strengthened them.

Now they're doing another rebirth around the world. They write, divine, encrypt graves and tombstones, bless ships, improve weapons, and perform magic.

But who am I? These are symbols, keys to Universal Creative Energy. These are energies that can be attracted and screened without regard to distance or time can be used to restore your life.

The Age of Aquarius, into which we just entered, gave us the laws of quantum physics. These laws prove that runes are energy, and can be used to improve your life.

Simply put, the laws of quantum physics tell us that there is an infinite ocean of ideas, intelligent energy called the quantum ocean. Spiritually it is the spirit of God, The Creator. God, who created all the gods.

There is no time or space in the quantum ocean right here- now.

Everything that has ever been is, or will be contained in the runes of the quantum ocean. There is and always has been.

The quantum ocean reacts to our thoughts and symbols. What you think or what Symbol you use connects you directly to the corresponding energy in the Quantum Ocean.

Therefore, runes are a symbol of the creative energies of the universe, contained in the quantum ocean.

For starters, meditate on each of the eighteen runes of Armanen Futhark. In this way, you draw the energy of runes into your aura. Any energy you carry in your aura attracts your life to you.

Don't worry about rune History, rune mythology, rune monuments, etc. Take one rune a day, watch and meditate for 15 minutes. Take care of only one keyword per Rune, so you know exactly what energy you attract to your aura.

Chapter 4

The Ancient Art of Runes Divination

Runes are a future prediction tool based on the ancient Germanic alphabet known as "Elder Futhark." The word "rune" is a derivative of the

Anglo-Saxon word meaning "mystery." Runes were used throughout Scandinavia, Germany, and some parts of Europe as early as 300 BC and remained in use until the 13th century when Latin replaced them.

The runic alphabet is probably a derivative of the ancient Etruscan Alphabet, which flourished in Italy since 600BC. In the fourth century, The Etruscan Alphabet was visually primitive and was characterized by angular lines and simple geometric shapes. Their straight lines allowed them to easily carve stones or cut wood.

Historically they were runes used as symbols for specific concepts or phrases that were most commonly associated with the natural world. Each rune had a coherent story.

These stories were based on the myths of the Nordic gods.

Today runes are mainly used as a method of divination. Like tarot reading, the practice of drawing runes from a set, and interpreting their meanings with a particular problem or concern. Each rune has its interpretation, and special meaning, based on esoteric concepts. As tarot reading, the more runes are drawn, the more complex reading.

When working with racing, it is also useful to ask open questions. Runes tend to be an excellent source for exploring problems or challenges, especially if you have concerns about the direction or measures to be taken in order to achieve the desired results.

It is important to note that the division of runes is not immutable, nor is it always predictable for the future.

For execution practices, the future is always perceived as a change, especially when someone is ready to incorporate specific actions.

However, the runes will help you to reveal the influences of the past, the nuances of the current situation, and the future course or potential outcome of the situation. Rune practitioner focuses on the cause and effect of runes used as a way to discover potential results, possible solutions, and key features that you need to understand their current tests.

Chapter 5

Reading the Runes a Contemporary Oracle From Viking Times

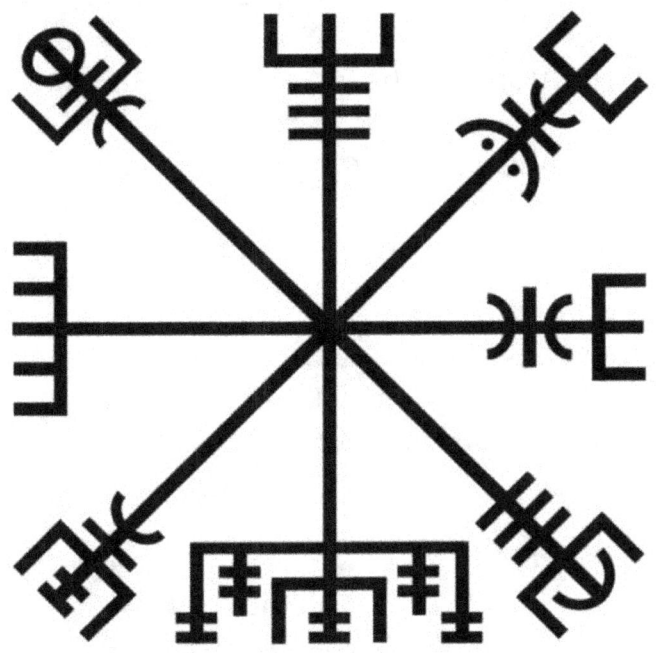

Runes are 25 stone objects, each with a printed character, except one which is an empty rune. Most runes come with a book that will help you unlock their meaning. As with tarot cards, no one knows who invented the runes or what their original meanings were. We know they were born with Vikings and crossed the Atlantic, but that's all.

Runes are fortune tellers. That means they won't tell you what to do in your life. What they do is emphasize the hidden motivations and personal choices that need to be addressed for progress in the current situation. Sometimes the information is pretty direct.

Sometimes you need to think about what you read to fully understand and accept the solution.

A typical use of runes

I recently waited for a friend to help me with a routine job.

So I drew a rune to examine the situation. Have you forgotten? Are you mad at me? Is he incompetent? I had no idea. So I asked: "why did he give up his sight when I needed it?" Then I reached into the bag and shot Rune # 23, "stopped."

The juice of the meaning was this:

"You may be powerless to do anything, but submit or surrender "Positive success is now unlikely

"All your plans await

"There is no reason for anxiety

"What you are experiencing is not necessarily the result of your actions

The next Monday, I found out why he didn't show up, didn't call, and let me ask. He had a migraine that happened on Thursday night and had no control until Sunday night.

See how I was Helpless to do anything It was obvious that

A positive result was unlikely and All my plans waited.

It was nice to know in advance that there is No reason for anxiety

And that

What I experienced was not the result of my actions; in other words, he wasn't mad at me; it was another reason why he didn't call. Instead of my brain floated from fear to rationalization to anger and back, I could take a deep breath and wait to hear all about it.

Hidden Patterns

My external motivation was to fulfill a task that I could not do myself, and that my friend offered to help.

My inner motivation was my desire to reproach him for not achieving my goal. He must be an unscrupulous friend if he lets me hang like that. I can't trust him. He's fragile.

Another internal motivation was to be a poor, sad victim of a ruthless friend. How could he do this to me? How can you call yourself my boyfriend when he treats me like that? I'm useless. The only friends I can attract are unscrupulous egotists.

The purposes of this discussion are, of course, exaggerated, but if you have enough poke, sometimes you'll notice that these so-called exaggerated statements are not far.

I had to choose between being a victim and/or blaming him, just waiting and not judging. The benefit is that I've released all my anxiety and anger to apply myself to more constructive things. In the meantime, he contacted me, did our job, and nobody got hurt.

Contemporary Rune

Tarot cards can be drawn from about 1500 AD. Runes date back to 1300 BC, bronze age. As mentioned above, no one knows the original meaning of runes. The first known references that were made about runes were written 1400 years after they were sculpted for the first time.

Enter Ralph Blum, author. Sometime before 1982 (not specified when exactly) has received a number of homemade runes, which were baked in the oven, like cookies. They were made by an English woman, who also provided her with two sheets of paper on which the alleged meanings were written. As it happens in life, he closes them and forgets about them, only to rediscover them one night and begin to try to understand them. If you're wondering if Ralph

Blum invented runes and designed the spread, well, yes, he invented it. But let me say that it was inspired, having in mind the meaning of runes. I think not, because it was a method used to unlock the meaning of modern runes that have less value as a tool. After all, many of Thomas Edison's best inventions came to him in dreams and are no less practical. Let's get rid of our disbelief and see what the runes bring us.

Before You Start

To use the rune, you do not need to perform any ritual. Get in the bag. But before you do this, concentrate, form a complete and concrete question in your mind. You should write it down first. The exact wording of your question can often convince you of the correct answer. Don't start with an awkward question like, "Should I quit?"Choose something less intense for your first exercise.

Draw a rune using a specific question

Think about it. Do not assume that the runes know what you mean. Put your hand in the bag and shake the runes. One of them will attack. I know it sounds funny, but over time, you know that feeling. Pull this rune out of the bag and put it vertically in front of you.

Remember that in the runes, there are inverted positions, so do not automatically rotate it one way or another. Just put the rune in front of you the way it looks. Now look in the book and read what it says.

Read the explanation, think about the formulation of your question. Think about the intent behind it, as we talked before. Trust, the runes takes a long time, so if you are not satisfied with your reading, you have three options: think about it, forget about it, or draw another.

That's my opinion that you should stay with Option # 1. Think. Give rune a chance to show you what she means to you. Also, sometimes, when you forget, the meaning will be revealed. I'm warning you not to draw another rune to confuse the problem. Over time, you will know when you should draw another rune, or even reverse the orientation of the rune, turning the head down or up, before or after reading the meaning.

There is another way to deal with runes. You can ask them to comment on the situation in your life. For example, when you pass your fingers through the stones in the bag, you can say, "the problem with the hand is my best friend." It's much more convenient than asking," Should I call my best friend for his terrible behavior? "Runes will look at the situation from all angles of view, and you need to study the answer to know what to do about a specific problem on the hand.

The beauty of Runeis that it makes you think. They give the responsibility to solve your problems firmly at your fingertips. And although we have lost the original meanings, their current meaning is practical and piercing. They even self-regulate. If you use them too often, instead of using your judgment and ideas, their message becomes confusing. If you keep them on the most complex questions of your life, the runes will shine a light on you.

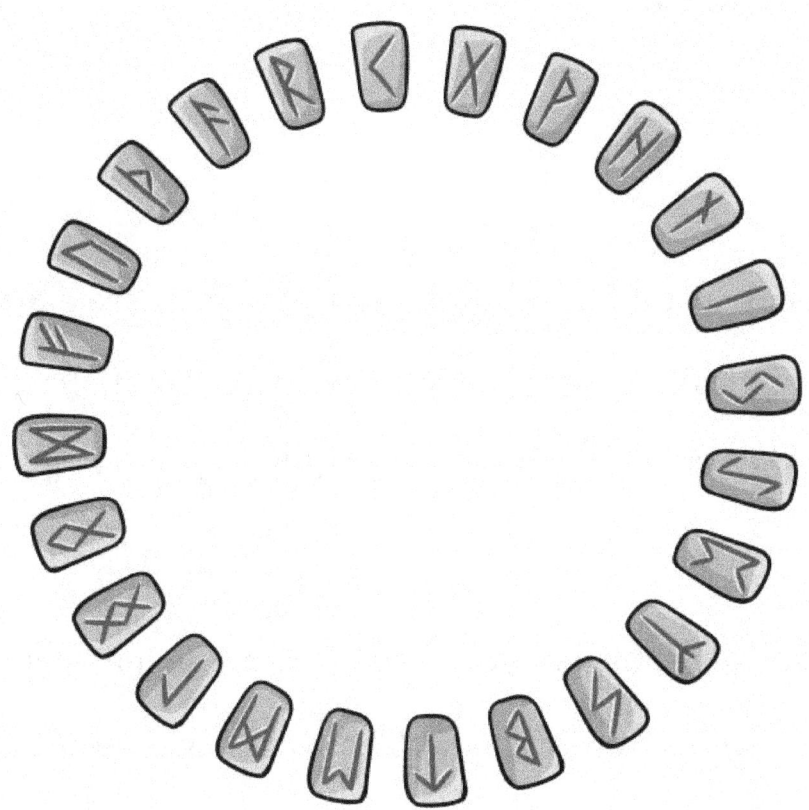

Chapter 6

Tips About Runes

Runes are not a predictive tool; they cannot and will not give future predictions, but they are more like an analytical tool, a proposal of possible results for the client, which may be in the middle of difficulty or problem.

Rune divisions provide client data through messages transmitted on each rune. These messages may seem confusing and meaningless at first, and therefore, many people who practice runes suggest that asking specific questions will provide a more detailed and specific answer.

In fact, runes, divination, reading can be complex, especially when you realize how many interpretations there are, some suggest keeping track of the measured values and results in a diary, so that the received messages can be easily understood.

Execution split values must be saved;

Date, time and method of casting Runic stones The questions you asked at the time

The order in which the runes land, for example, face up or down the meaning you took of the race

Your feelings and impressions of reading

Reading rune divination can be used in different ways, but there must be some basics in place to get the best possible result and Rune impressions. The most important thing is to focus before the beginning of the reading. In other words, it slows down the mind, the emptiness of fear and tension, etc. and opens the runes.

Many people meditate before using runes;

Many people use the cast " Yes / No."

That is, runes ask closed questions that can only cause a yes or no answer. Before asking questions about Run, customers need to focus, using the left rune to mix the runes.

After asking the question, the vertical rune answers "Yes," and the inverted runic stone means "no."

A cast of a rune or the casting of Odin

This casting is a quick and easy way to get an answer to a particular question. Many racing wheels use it every day after meditation. Focus on the question, which lasts one or two minutes, the rune is then launched, and the answer will be given.

There are many other runes that read divination, and casts that can be made, some much more complicated than the two singles mentioned above. The use of runes as a means of offering opinions or possible solutions to the problems that afflict our daily lives requires skills and understanding. Prevent people who claim to be experts at the rune wheel in a short time; using Rune is a skill that takes many years to win. It would be true to say that Runic wheels never stop learning stones.

Chapter 7

13 Steps to Rune Power

There are 13 steps to understand and practice before you can use all the rune power effects.

Runes are universal creative energy. Each rune is the key to creative energy. Example: rune fa= wealth, Rune Ur= health, Rune Thorn= protection, etc.

Now we are in the Age of Aquarius, which means that we are in the new S. T. E-mail. M. (space, time, energy, matter) continuum, in the Galaxy.

This new era has given us a new paradigm to work with. This paradigm is based on the laws of Quantum physics.

The laws of quantum physics tell us that there is an infinite ocean of ideas, of intelligent energy called quantum Ocean where everything that has ever been, is or will exist.

The runes and gods/goddesses of the North exist there and have always existed there.

We can contact and transfer the energy of the quantum ocean with our thoughts, symbols, and rituals.

Because thoughts are things that we literally "thought" in our current reality. To change our current place, we must change our thoughts.

Purpose 21st century, the age of the Rune Aquarius shaman, rune magician, and Rune guide is to go to the quantum ocean and bring the energy of the runes and gods/goddesses within an hour. Transfer their energy and strength to the present. Do not return to them in the past.

The playing field matrix, which must be used by the shaman, mage, magician, this is the spirit.

We are all in the spirit age. All the creations we see around us, religion, churches, politics, schools, technology, monuments, books, etc.

Now you, as Rune Shaman magician, a magician can use your mind to bring the energy of Rune and god/goddess to the north of the quantum ocean and create new structures for them. Modern.

The tools you use to do this are the power of runes. Bring this rune energy to your aura, life, and home. Protect your home by connecting it with runes.

Mentally contact the helpers you need, both spiritual and physical, to help you.

We can do it together. We can revive the energy of Rune, and our culture of Northern, and not return to the past, like many books of rune and Asatru, but bring the strength of the past to the hour.

Chapter 8

The Ancient Advice of Rune Readings

It is not uncommon for the media to use a tool for Fortune-Telling during reading. Fortune-telling tools help the reader to draw on the psychic sphere, or psychic energy of a particular person, place, or thing. One of the most popular Oracle tools that the Media uses are runes. Runes can penetrate, predict, and reflect. When you get a reading of a psychic rune, you can expect a reading full of wisdom and practical advice.

Runes are ancient symbols of the ancient Germanic alphabet known as "Elder Futhark." The term "rune" means "mystery." Runes were used throughout Scandinavia, Germany and some parts of Europe as early as 300 BC, when Christianity became commonplace, the practice of reading runes lost its popularity due to its association with paganism. Today, runes have become one of the most popular methods of divination. Not only are they accustomed to guessing the future, but they are also used in the work of Wiccan spells and rituals.

When reading psychic Runes, runes are used as a means of predicting the future. They can also be used to answer important questions or find solutions to difficult situations. Usually, the medium makes you pull the runes out of the bag and put them in front of you. How many runes to draw depends largely on the medium with which you work, and the specific spread of their choice. Similar to tarot cards, the media have different ways of interpreting runes and usually have a number of extended runes they prefer to work with.

Some clairvoyants force you to shoot a rune as a way to mentally connect with your energy. When this happens, the medium uses the rune as a magnet. Rune draws your energy into the material from which it is made (most often from Stone). The medium then holds the rune as a way to tune in its energy.

Runes can help the media to discover the effects of your past, the current energy of your present situation, and the future course, or the potential outcome of your future. Data from runes tend to focus on the cause and effect of your decisions and actions. A psychic will use the runes as a tool that will help you discover your future possibilities and the practical advice that you may need to work through their current challenges.

Chapter 9

Runes, Why Are They Becoming So Popular?

The Runes have a revival, as well as the Tarot.

These are ways to better understand our lives and look towards growing popularity, because we are trying to understand our lives in depth.

RuneHistory

Runes are ancient figures used in Teutonic, Anglo-Saxon, and Scandinavian civilizations, and are found on many ancient inscriptions.

They were probably used for the first time by the Eastern Goths (C.300), which are considered to be derived from the Greek-italic script. They were widely used throughout Europe, Iceland, England,

Ireland, and Scotland until the final establishment of Christianity.

After that, the use of runes was disgusted as a pagan practice, so their use was discouraged, interrupted, or used in secret. In Scandinavia, their use persisted even after the Middle Ages; they were used for manuscripts and inscriptions.

The word rune is derived from a First Anglo-Saxon word meaning, "secret or mystery."

Therefore, in our distant past, the writing was perhaps much more serious than today, not only to communicate, but it was full of magical power.

Runes were often used to cast spells on someone who loves you, or make an enemy helpless or even die.

Interestingly, when casting spells, the writing of runes was accompanied by whispers (whispers) or prayers or curses, also called Runes. It was to make effective magic.

Today, the renaissance of the runes, which as a whisper disappeared, reappeared from the fog of the past.

The Runes have now been rediscovered as a significant symbolic system and have gained a wide track as a means of divination.

In addition to the Tarot, they give an insight into the past and future, as they allow understanding the life and beliefs of our ancestors.

Runes can teach us something about a way of life that was more intimately related to the worlds of nature and spirit than ours today.

The darkest period in the history of the study of the runes was paradoxically their revival by German scholars associated with the Nazi movement at the age of 20 and 30.

The legitimate historical research of our past has unfortunately been overshadowed by Nazi propaganda and racism, and the results are negligible.

However, the runes appeared in our cultural sphere, and with it came its secret, and perhaps power.

Today, runes are basically used as a method of divination.

However, since there are no reliable historical descriptions of Runic divination (at least not known to the general or academic community), virtually any chosen method can be considered valid.

There are some rune features that make them more suitable for some methods than others.

Most runes, for example, are cut into small pieces of wood, clay, or stone. They are designed to be easily pick up and scattered, rather than being set according to a particular pattern (like the Tarot)

How Runes are used.

You must either buy a set of them (sold in bookstores or stores or New Age sites). You can make your own. You're going to need a bag to put them in. There are several good books to buy that will explain all these steps in detail.

However, as an example, after you have your runes, you can quickly ask yourself a few questions mentally, then put his hand in the bag and pull out three runes as in the system below.

Norns System (The Three-Sleeve Easy Casting).

This method is useful for obtaining an overview and giving an idea of the future result.

The result will depend on how much time and effort you put into analyzing and understanding the meaning of each rune.

To begin with, you take a rune out of the bag and put it face down. This rune represents the first Norn or those events in the past that affect the current situation.

Remove the next race and place it next to the first. This is the second Norn or the current situation, which often requires a choice.

Pull a third and put it down. This is the third Norn and often turns out to be the most difficult rune to interpret. Can represent the inevitable fate of man, or it can just be the final result, if the current situation remains unchanged, or even one or more results.

You need to rely on your own psychic abilities to decide what the answer is. As in all things, exercise makes perfect. It is something that the more you exercise and concentrate, the better the result.

Chapter 10

Rune Crystals

Runes are the key to the universal creative energy contained in the quantum ocean. Each Rune unlocks the separate energy with all its harmonic attributes.

Now, thanks to the laws of quantum physics, we can draw the runic energy from the quantum ocean and our auras. Any energy we carry in our auras draws us to our physical reality.

Looks like a meeting. Fa Rune is the energy of wealth. Breathe in your aura and attract wealth into your life. Well, with all the runes.

Crystals are very magical in their own way. They are conscious and exist in their own kingdom. Everything in our physical universe is a manifestation of the energy matrix in the quantum ocean. Crystals have their own energy world in the quantum ocean and in their particular universe.

The main property of crystals is that they can be used as tools for energy concentration.

The symbolism of the Rune 18 Futhork is based on the geometry of the hexagon and its diameter. The strength of quartz crystal is also based on a hexagon.

Put these two together, and you will have a huge concentrated power. The final strength of the crystals is obtained by combining them with 18 Sacred Runes of Futhork.

The ancient masters of Rune knew how to use the energy of the world crystal with the help of runes. They even used a hexagonal crystal consisting of ice and snow.

Each rune is a partial energy of a large world, Crystal, which contains all the energies.

The rituals and practices of Rune Crystals are very strong. The secret of using crystals with runes was a secret that was kept for a long time by ghosts, Alchemists, and magicians of the world. Karl Welz knows this information, and you can go to his website and get an introduction to these powerful practices.

If you look at the pure quartz crystal from above, you will see Rune Hagal. All runes are seen from different angles in the Crystal.

The sacred geometry of the circle, ellipses, pyramids, and hyperbole is located in the cone. Conical sections represent planetary, Galactic, and intergalactic orbits. They represent the energy of the universe, from the atom to the Galaxy.

To work effectively with crystal magic and runes, you will need to create a set of engraved crystals of one rune each.

Then you will have a powerful tool that will enhance your rune work in healing magic and spirituality. For healing work, you need to know the correlation between runes and spiritual anatomy.

Rune mantras, Rune Yoga, rune meditation, and Rune breathing are enhanced with the help of Rune Crystals.

Chapter 11

The Way Psychics Use Runes

The use of clairvoyants has been going on for many centuries. In fact, this is an ancient form of writing, which was used by many Nordic countries before the

Roman alphabet, which we know today. It is believed that the runes were brought to Britain around the fifth century.

If you look at the history of the rune, you will find that the word rune is interpreted as a mystery or a whisper. Around the runes, there are various myths and stories.

Myths and stories include how Runes should have become magical. I use a series of runes that I made of gems. The fact is that for me, this is just a concentrated tool.

Psychic abilities usually work. The only time I shoot is when I'm really in the reading space that I usually have to do in a chat room.

This brings me back to the spiritual connection. Usually, runes focus me on the area my mental abilities need to focus on. The runes themselves are very interesting.

When I made mine, I learned a lot about them just by painting a rune on a stone. I think when you do runes, you will fill some of your spirits with a rune. It's the work of love, making your own tools.

These figures, which are painted on stones, wood, or other media, were like these ancient peoples of the alphabet, as well as their divine instrument. At some point in history, people were persecuted for using runes and even burned at the stake.

The current type of Rune commonly used is actually called FuThark. There are 24 runes that are organized into three families. Each of the families is led by their Nordic god. These gods are Freya & Frey, Heindall, and Tyr. The meaning of runes is open to psychic interpretation, and this is something that everyone must learn on their own. When using runes according to tradition, you should throw them on a white canvas.

Once the fabric is laid, make sure of the direction you go. It should be towards the sun. Now throw rocks in the sun right out of the box or the case where you are holding them.

Some will face it, and some will not. The runes that have their symbols are the ones you will read for the querent. Read them from left to right.

Those on the left are read first. Read exactly as they are shown. They must be read inverted or upright, depending on how they land. Only at this stage, your psychic abilities come into play.

It's an interesting tool to use, and you should make time for your own if you want to do it. Any clairvoyant will appreciate how they bring your intuition to the fore.

Chapter 12

How to Use Rune Secrets for Survival

Runic Survival

These are very difficult times for the culture of the peoples of northern Europe. The world is painted with a large brush and only one color. Everyone is forced to wear a 9 1/2 size shoe, whether it fits or not.

But this idea is an idea that belongs to a bygone age. They belong to the age of fish, the age of breeding, all in one system of faith. But it can not stand, because the fate of mankind is governed by higher laws, not by laws politically correct.

We have abandoned the age of fish that has dominated the minds and lives of humanity for the last 2,000 years.

We have just entered the age of Aquarius, which will last for another 2,000 years. This is the age of the mind, the age of individualism, the age of thinking, and the creation of one's own reality.

But we've just entered a new era. We've been in it for less than 100 years. The power and wisdom of this new era are very young and not powerful.

The thoughts of the dinosaurs of the fish age are still very strong, and as a dying dinosaur, it takes time to fall dead. But it will be. That's the law. Just don't let it fall on you when it collapses.

As the nations of Northern Europe, we have one of the most powerful tools on the planet to use for our survival in these difficult times. They're the secret of our runes. Runes are universal creative energy. Each rune represents an individual kind of energy.

It's time to get the Runic energies into our auras, so they will not only serve as protective shields against modern society, but also attract a new reality for you.

The new paradigm of this age of Aquarius is summarized in the laws of quantum physics. These laws tell us that there is an endless ocean of thought energy that responds to our thoughts and symbols.

Runes exist and have always existed in the quantum ocean. It's time to think outside the quantum ocean and in your lives; In your auras, to be more precise. This is one of the secrets of runes.

These are the energies that you can attract and use in your daily life, not for prophecy, but for protection and creation.

Rune Secret: What Rune energy we carry in our auras attracts our life to us.

In order to survive this dangerous time, we need to pull the energy of the FA, Uraz, and mandrel from the quantum ocean.

Rune FA is the energy of prosperity. Attracting energy from the quantum ocean and in your aura, you begin to attract prosperity into your life.

Rune URAZ is a rune of health. We all need more money and better health to survive this time. SLANDER is the rune of energy comes into your Aura and then infuse energy throughout the body, slowly but surely leads to better health.

Rune THORN is a rune of protection. We need protection from all sorts of evil people, places, and events. We also need protection from mental and electronic risks.

The best way to get the energy of these three runes, health, wealth, and protection from the quantum ocean and in your life, is to meditate on them and breathe them.

Secret Rune: every morning for half an hour, sit quietly in your favorite chair. Take one rune at a time. Meditate on it. Start attracting Runic energy for (health, wealth, and protection) from the quantum Ocean into your aura and life.

Triplicate.

Then get Up and continue your business with the confidence of knowing that you just started runic power (health, wealth, and protection) in your life.

Repetition is God's first law. Tomorrow, start with a long repetition of life. Do this, and you will survive this change for centuries.

Chapter 13

Psychic Runes

The word rune means, "whisper, secret or mystery." Each of them translates into phrases or words that indicate the spirit and forces of nature. Each race has a relationship with the Nordic god, which is represented by history. Psychic runes are essentially a fortune teller who gives advice to those who ask for it.

The story of the emergence of the psychic runes goes like this. Odin, who is the Northern Supreme God of Aesir, was impaled on his spear. He clung to Yggdrasil, a tree of the world, nine days and nights to gain the knowledge needed to understand the runes. When the runes appeared, he collected them and acquired the knowledge that gave him power. Later he passed this knowledge on to Freya, the Goddess Vanir. In return, he taught her the magic of seidra. Humanity received the knowledge of the runes of Heimdall, The Guardian of the Rainbow Bridge.

To become qualified as a psychic rune launcher, you need to cultivate your knowledge of the culture, mythology, and history of ancient Scandinavia and Europe. Rune lore is closely related to them. This knowledge shows you in the right direction, but the depth to which you study depends on you.

Throwing a psychic rune is not a prophecy because you do not see the future. They will only give you one way to analyze the path you are looking for and what the result might be. Remember, the future is not fixed. Everything you do changes the future in a way. If you do not like where you are going, you always have the opportunity to change the result of your actions and decisions.

The best way to ask psychic runes for advice is to explain your situation in detail. When you do, ask me a specific question. Sometimes the results are not very clear. They may suggest answers, but you need to understand the details.

The best way to read psychic runes is to clear your mind of everything except the question you want to ask. Focus on her.

When you focus on the issue and feel ready, choose a rune. This will help you gather the information you need to answer the question you have in mind. If you think you need more information, collect three runes instead of just one. The first will provide you with information about the circumstances of your request.

The second shows the way forward. The third will give you a result if you go down this path. Remember, choose your last route. You can control your future. Take your time and choose wisely.

Runes used in Psychic Reading

Runes are used for hundreds of years, and the use of these in a psychic reading can give you both the wisdom and the understanding of the problem, which may be in your aura right now. Each symbol on a rune stone has a special meaning, and it is amazing how accurately they tend to portray the current situation.

Runes come from the northern regions and tend to have names like Jera, which is the equivalent of the wheel of fortune when cards or Runes sowulo, which is like Sun cards. Everyone has a little story about the runes; you need to learn to interpret not only on its own, but in combination with the other runes drawn at the same time. Again, your psychic abilities are encouraged to use for both interpretation and guidance in the area of concentration, as weaving a psychic reading to present to the client. For everyone, you can make your own runes and print cards. I made both wooden runes and stones from various semiprecious stones.

Look inside and find your answer, and that's really what you have to do. Use your psychic intuition. In addition to direct meanings, there are also inverse meanings for many runes, but not all of them. For example, Jera has no opposite meaning, because, in both directions, it looks the same.

The same goes for Sowul, but Algiz has both. In a vertical position, try not to use your assets or goods to protect themselves, but in the same way, do not put a picture of myself on the world and do not insulate yourself from the world in general. When this reverses, it tells you that it's time to let go of the protection you used, because it creates a barrier for your growth. The use of Runic stones can give you a great overview, both standing and in the opposite position.

The use of these psychic Runic stones gives you the ability to connect to the mind and then give an intuitive reading to a certain depth. Once you know and understand the importance of the Rune, you will soon be fascinated by exactly how to touch the necessary points surrounding the person on which you focus.

Chapter 14

Rune Symbols

Since the beginning of the centuries, mankind has found fascinating and powerful signs and symbols. The power of race comes from what they have to teach us. Runes bring us lessons and, if used wisely, can facilitate the rapid and effective recovery of these lessons. Runes do not give answers to all life's problems.

They do not even fill their user with magical forces. They give signs on the way to life. Runes represent certain images, and in cooperation with them, leadership and teaching are accessible to everyone.

The tradition of run-casting was once the domain of the Chosen Few, and only a minority sought spiritual enlightenment. Today, many people are looking for answers to questions, and these seekers of wisdom should have access to clear instructions about this ancient oracle.

The track is soft but strong and has a profound effect on many levels. They are used not only for divination but also for protection, healing, strengthening, and learning. The mystery of runes is not a mystery; it's just a path to greater consciousness that anyone can pedal.

In order to learn runes, you need to tune in to their vibrations. Each rune has a matching tree, color, grass, and Crystal, which are keys that unlock your lessons. When working with them, you can define a field of vibrations that will allow the subconscious to learn vibrations and give a lesson to the conscious mind. Instead of a conscious mind trying to find the lesson of each rune, you can allow the lesson to find you.

If you want to know runes, it is important to make your own set, rather than a ready-made purchase. It may take time and energy, but it will give you a much more intimate relationship with your runes. Runes are usually made of two materials, wood and stone, but you can use other materials, such as crystals, glass balls, or clay.

The process of creating your runes is quite long, and I'm not going to go there, there are some very important steps that you must complete before you can use your settings.

The Geometric Forms of Rune Symbols are Energies

Rune-Vibration

The age of Aquarius gave us the laws of quantum physics. The laws of quantum physics tell us that everything is energy. Energy is vibration. Runes are creative energy or universal vibration. Your physical body is a configuration of vibration or energy.

The only real thing that actually happens in the universe is the infinite scale (from top to bottom), energy (vibration) in relationships.

The key to the term study is to create a relationship between the energy of running it and the energy of your physical body. The energy of your physical body can be summed up as an Aura. Every energy you bring to your Aura will attract people, places, and events into your life. So learn to attract the energy you want.

This is called the law of attraction. Select a particular rune and transfer its energy (vibration) to your aura. Attract a physical race counterpart.

Use FA runes and attract wealth. Rune UR-salute. Rune plug- protection. The shape of each rune creates a different force, shape, and function. The real geometric outline of the tracks is a vibration. Rune Chuck has the protective power, shape, and function of Rune Chuck to protect them. Well, it's with all the runes.

In fact, all forms emit vibrations. Squares, circles, balls, trapezoids, etc. all of them have a special energy.

The runic position of the body of yoga is also a vibration of form. By practicing running, you draw the energy of rune to your aura.

Train while you are in the running position. Begin to realize the runic currents of energy that enter your body. It enters your left hand, flows through your body, and leaves with your right hand.

Do the same with rune or with another rune. When you accept specific visions and feelings, write them down in your magic diary.

Rune mantras are also living forms. Sit in your favorite chair and continuously sing the rune mantras for at least five minutes (the more, the better). Write down all the visions and feelings in your book.

Use the yoga rune position and remove the energy from the rune with your hands as you sing. While you do this, expect the runes to set in motion everything you need to achieve your goals. You can also practice the position of the runes yoga points lying on the floor. The key to attracting the power of the runes is training.

Chapter 15

Using Runes for Divination

There are various methods and tools of divination that have existed since the earliest times. Men have guessed the questions and anything to divination, which can be applied using cow shells, divination stones, pendulum, among others. Runes are used for divination, in fact, are very common and have 26 stones, each stone has a printed symbol, and each of the symbols has its own meaning and interpretation, which are used to predict what the future will bring. These divination stones are used in the same way as African cow shells are used for divination by African astrologers.

Each of the Stones has its own meaning and the meaning can be interpreted to predict the future, however, when some of the Stones co-occur together, or when they appear in a specific pattern, the co-occurrence of some of the Stone gives a completely different meaning, and the pattern in which the stones occur can also be interpreted so as to give divination.

Use runes to predict the future is not something that is completely shrouded in mystery, If you are wondering how to use these tools for divination, and you also want to become a psychic, there are certain qualifications that you need to be able to use them, as well as divination does not include many more complex rituals

In order to be able to use stones for divination, you must own your own runes; now, having your own runes is a fairly easy task. You can buy in the local store of art supplies. However, if you want these stones to be really personal and strong, there is nothing to beat to make the stones yourself. You may think that it will be a complex process, but the opposite is true and the formation of the stones themselves, adds a personal touch to the stones.

The best runes are often made from a flat stone, which you can easily get to the beach; however, if you are able to get such stones, another group of flat stones will do all the time, which brings you as close to nature as possible. If these stones do not have access to even the most important pieces of wood, they should be able to keep the mark, which for them will be made.

Chapter 16

What Can Norse Mythology Teach You About Runes?

In my eyes, it is impossible to understand the true nature of runes without studying Nordic mythology. A common mistake of modern "rune masters" is that they study runes in terms of using divination, and not the old tradition. But the inhabitants of the North used runes in different ways; the practice of divination was only part of it.

It is important that every aspiring rune master remember that if you want to master Nordic runes, you must read Nordic mythology, explore Poetic Edda, and Northern sagas. What can he teach you? I would say a lot of things.

For example, I have learned many different runic spells and rituals, which have not been described in any of the rune books I have ever encountered; therefore, I believe that their authors have never really studied the mythology behind the runes. Many interesting uses of runes in spells and high magic can be found in the Poetic Edda itself. For more information, see the classic sagas. For example, no Rune book I've read has ever mentioned that Thurisaz's rune can be used to induce mental illness.

Another interesting thing that you can find with the help of Nordic mythology is the correspondence between runes and Scandinavian gods. For example, while most books on runes agree that Thurisaz is the rune of the god Thor, I have not found many books that mention that Heimdall was the God of Daguz and a few other runes. Or that Nauthiz, Isa, and Hagalaz are runes "guarded" by Nornes- Urd, Werdandi, and Skult. This leads to the interesting interpretation that the Hagalaz guarded by Urd is the rune of the past; Nauthiz guarded by the Rune of Skuld's future and Isa, guarded Werdandim, is the rune of the present. It can be used in many different divinatory and magical practices.

Exploring Nordic mythology is not only fun but also educational for anyone interested in runes.

You can find explanations of each rune, descriptions of spells and rituals, and examples of uses for each rune, scripts, and bindrunes. It is important to remember that mastering the subject of running requires not only the learning of Runes, but also the culture where they come from - the culture of Vikings and people who precede. Without it, no one can become a real Runemaster

Rune Berkana + Norse Goddess Frigga + Quantum Physics = Protection For Home And Children

Frigga is the goddess of northern Europe of home, fertility, love, motherhood, and protection.

Women with or without children need the protective vibrations of the Goddess Friggy and the energy of her powerful Rune Berkana in their lives and homes. The chaotic and destructive energies of the media and politically correct societies are trying to destroy the home, family, and role of women in Northern Europe.

Protect yourself, your children, and your home. Avoid these destructive energies with periodic frying spots. Also a strong relationship with the goddess Frigga herself.

Runes and Northern goddesses are still very powerful, and only by bringing them to your house, they will have a healing effect and serve as a protective bumper. How many millions of people have

crosses, icons, and Moonlight in their homes for protection? As Northern Europe, we also need our powerful symbols and icons.

FRIGGA RUNES

With the goddess Frigga, three runes are connected.
Runa Fehu

Runa Perth

Runa Berkana

Rune Berkana Is The Rune Of Women.

In this stain, we want protection for women and the House. We only use a rune in this place, Berkana Rune. It is very powerful and will act as a magic amulet for you, your children, and your home.

The Goddess Frigga

Frigga is the mother of Odin, his wife.

She is the goddess of Home, Family, fertility, love, motherhood, Home Affairs, and easy transition (dying.)

Frigga is as powerful as Odin and is the only God/Goddess who can sit in the high seat of Odin when there is none. From there, he can look at the whole universe. There's nothing you don't know. But she's called the silent goddess because she doesn't talk about what she knows.

Friggin's sons are Thor, Balder, and Hodar.

His stepchildren are Heimdal, Tyr, Vidan, and Skljoldr.

The Orion constellation belt is known as Friggy's Qutaff. The rotating stars at night are his spinning wheel. They say Frigga uses his spinning wheel to weave clouds. At the beginning of each New Year, he also sits at the spit, weaving the fate of people and gods.

If you want, ask Friggy your fate before building a relationship with her and her Rune Berkana. He could tell you. But be careful. He knows all the destinies of men, women, and gods. He knew the fate of his son Balder. He knew he was going to die, and proving how he was going, with all your powers, couldn't stop him. Do you really want to Know Your Fate? Ask. I like to leave my work alone.

The name Frigg means love. He lives in Fensalir, which means "salt marshes."

In Scandinavia, Frigge's blessing still evokes the birth of women with a white candle, with a Berkan rune engraved on the side. The candle is used as a charm to ensure safe delivery.

Girls Hand Frigga

Eir - - - - - goddess of healing. Clay, goddess of protection.

GNA - - - - - - Messanger Dea. Fulla - - - - - goddess of fertility.

Also LOFN, SJOFN, son, GEFJON, SNORTA, VAN and VOR.

Ask yourself: Why do you want to make a frying pan for stains? Why do you want to fry in your life?

In the more than 100 pages I have written about races and spots,

there is a repeated theme. Be focused.

Each goddess has different powers and functions, as well as each rune. During washing, choose a rune, a goddess, a keyword in which you pour your mental energy. Thus, energies are stored in the quantum Ocean (the spirit of God), where all energies exist. The more accurate you are with your thoughts about what you want to do, the stronger and more successful the stain will be.

The laws of quantum physics have taught us that ideas are things. Our thoughts are projected into the quantum ocean (Divine Spirit), where the creative energy collected and materialize it in our lives.

You need to pay attention to what you think and what you do. You need to know why you want to bring Frigge energy into your life.

There's nothing the goddesses can do for us. That's not how it works. What works is for you to attract the energy the goddess has used in the quantum ocean

(Divine Spirit) and your life. You cannot become a Frigga, but you can become a Frigga.

You can recover your life using the goddess runes that are universal creative energy and the laws of quantum physics, which tells us that thoughts are things.

We, The Northern Europeans, discovered the runes, the laws of quantum physics and the laws of mental radionics. We will use them to create a better world for us and our children and grandchildren. Our children are our most precious possessions.

Use tracks to create.

Call Frigg For Berkan's Race.

Frigga is the goddess of women. I can only share it with you because I'm a man and she won't tell me. But as a woman, you can build (and should build in these chaotic times) a strong relationship with her. She can't share her secrets with you.

Whatever problems a woman may have, stress and fears, dishonest relationships, etc. cause Frigg. Invoke it to ensure an easy and perfect delivery. Use the ritual white candle. It is recommended to place on the abdomen, the symbol of the Rune Berkana.

But especially in today's chaotic world, your children and your home need the protection of Friggy and Rune Berkana.

Frigga Blot Ritual

The Vikings will not help us with their axes and swords. Our minds, our runes, and our Sciences do it.

This is for women who want to work alone in the privacy of their modern home, with 21 rituals. You will draw Frigg's protective energy using the Berkan rune, quantum ocean (god's spirit), and in your aura.

Let's get started.

Sit quietly in your favorite armchair. Relax. Hold the Berkan rune (print it from the bottom of the page) on your knees. Look and meditate on it. Your mind (mental radionic) will create a connection between Fry Runic energies in the quantum ocean (god's spirit) and you.

Breathe deeply and breathe in the Berkan energy. Use your imagination to see these white protective energies flowing from the Friga to the quantum ocean for you.

Mentally intone to yourself:

"I am now inspired by the energy of the Berkan Frigg runes of the quantum Ocean (the spirit of God) and in my aura.

Expire.

Inspiration and intonation. Expire.

Inspiration and intonation. Expire.

Three times three magic is a figure of the gods and goddesses of the North.

Your aura is now filled with the protective energy of friggin Berkan rune.

Relax and enjoy its peaceful and healing energies.

Take a deep breath and exhale. At the same time, it displays the protective energy of the Friga, which comes out of the Pinal gland (third eye) in the center of the forehead. Here is a very strong secret that few people know or practice. Each organ of our body has a special function. Our pituitary gland at the top of our heads is to receive higher energy, such as outgoing energy or the quantum Ocean (the spirit of God. Our pineal gland in the middle of our forehead is to send this energy to the physical world.

Modern doctors know very little about these two spiritual glands because they have lost their spirituality. The Curse of our time. To use this as an analogy: we receive the powerful energy of God, from the quantum ocean and at the top of our heads, to our pituitary gland. We distribute this energy in the physical world through the pineal gland.

As mentioned above, below.

All great magicians, healers, and shamans know. Only now, thanks to the discovery of the laws of quantum physics, we have it. While mentally pouring energy from the intoning pineal gland.

"I send protective energy to surround my house and land with a ball of white light."

Look at your whole house and gardens surrounded by Frigg's protective white light.

Three times.

Take a deep breath and exhale this protective light to each of your children and grandchildren.

Intoned:

"I send Frigg's protective energies to surround him (name) and protect him all day."

Three times for each child and grandson. Mentally thank Frigg and do your job with confidence that you, your home, your children, and grandchildren are protected.

Chapter 17

The Origin and Purpose Behind the Ancient Symbols and Alphabet

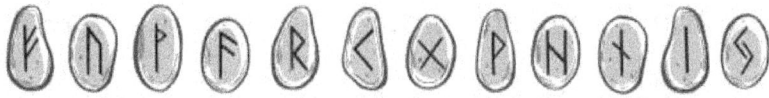

SCANDINAVIAN RUNES

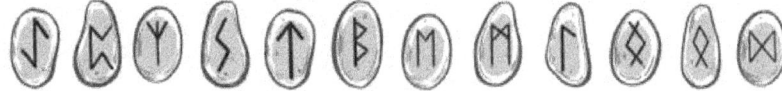

Ask six rune experts: "where do these runes come from? And you'll probably have six different answers. There are different versions of runes for every culture and ERA from which they seemed to come. One person told me they came from the Vikings, another said they came from the Druids, another said they came from other people, each person is serious and thought they had the right origins of the runes, how can each have a different answer to them?

The answer seems to be "time." Over the years, people have created so many stories about the runes that no one knows their true origin. The word "rune" is a word derived from the Gothic word" rune," which means "mystery."

One of the oldest and earliest recorded uses of runes came from German tribes in central and Eastern Europe after the first use of runes show that they were not even meant to be a language for everyday speech, but were used as a symbolic alphabet system. Each letter or form of runes had its own sound and meaning; in fact, each rune represented a deity, or the so-called God, who gave it its special power. People in the past believed that by carving the runes into their belongings, or other objects, the God or deity of the rune would protect the object, they even believed that a sword could be more powerful for use in battle by carving the runes.

There are at least six different types of runes or runic alphabet, which people use, or dabble with today, and every runic alphabet should be the correct settings to use, if you ask the person who uses them.

Runes have no special meaning other than symbols, drawings or characters, if you do not have the belief that they are magical, and they will, they are nothing but drawing a circle or a square, and gives them a special meaning.

For example, when I was walking around for hundreds of years, maybe I looked in the direction of the sun in the sky, and then drew or carved circle on a stone or a piece of wood. For me, that meant a lot, a powerful circle that lights the fire in the sky. To someone else years later, that my circle carved into the stone, you may think that the circle represents the wheel, an eye, a month, or just a simple circle. Each person uses runes for their own purposes, and each person gives them their own meaning.

In ancient Europe, it seemed that many adults produced wood carvings; in fact, it was a valuable skill handed down from one family member to another. It was required, the alphabet that can be easily sculpted or engraved in the wood used by sculptors. Runes are for the ideal because they consist mainly of straight lines, which are connected to each other.

Most of the rune used was nothing more than a trademark that symbolized a trademark or possessed an object. Then they were modified, and more symbols were added as the country's population increased, and its language skills required more symbols and meanings.

The runes were and are written in different ways, by different people, some are written from left to right, others are written from right to left, or from top to bottom, shows once again that the runes have different meanings for different people.

Today, many people think that runes were used for magic or divination and prediction of the future; it still depends on the person who reads such meanings in the rune. Years ago, when the Christian faith was adopted in Europe, the use of runes fell and was replaced by the more modern Roman/Latin alphabet, in fact, the letter of the Latin alphabet also contains an earlier rune symbol as part of the language.

Years later, when Christianity spread, the use of the runes fell, the leaders of the church did not understand their meaning and symbols, in such a way that they are considered the evil, or the devil, is the thought that continued today.

This is the basis of the idea that modern occultists, druids, and New-agers even Hitler, in his twisted thinking, that the use of the symbols of the runic alphabet in the Nazi military insignia must give his army more power. This, of course, turned out to be stupid, because other military forces crushed the Nazi regime.

But still, many people like to use runes today because they are ancient objects; they have a mystical and even occult power for some people. I say, use it for fun, do not try to use them for divination or spells, all this is clearly against the true source of power, the power of God and his son Jesus Christ. In fact, to show you the weakness of the race of Prophecy, the modern rune contains a white rune; the White rune symbolizes the unknowable.

Do you not think a great source of knowledge or power to know everything? Once again, look at the Bible and Jesus Christ for your future, this is the only book of prophecy that has been and will continue to be, 100% accurate.

Some of the runes commonly used today are: "Elder Futhark," "Younger Futhark," "the Anglo-Saxon Futhorc," "Robert "rune," after "Robert." Runes have become very popular because it is the only version of the runes that includes a full translation of the English alphabet, which makes it possible to write any English text in runes. Robert executions are also available as "true type font" for use on any Windows computer.

Chapter 18

Secret Of Using Runes During The Correct Month For Rune Magic

ARMANEN RUNE AND SEASONS

For a place stronger magic runes during the months where they are stronger and perform magic Rune during that month. There is a time and a place for everything.

This is important for those of you who want to practice Rune Magic.

To become a good racing assistant, you need to learn everything about energy. Rune energy, the energy of seasons, energy of individual months, trees, plants, colors, sounds, etc.

AND THAT YOU HAVE TO DO YOURS. ANYTHING YOU WANT TO USE FOR YOUR MAGIC.

Otherwise, you just play with runes. It's not shit. It is used by the most powerful people in the world.

Companies use it in advertising, in their slogans, in their music, in the images you present on TV and in the magazine. Politicians, religious leaders use black magic. It is very thin, but very thick.

Learn how to use rune magic to protect your family from other spells.

The next thing you need is to train Bindrune Magic:

PATIENCE

Plan your Bindrune Magic; choose the right day, month, or time of year. Take your time.

Rune FA - - - - - 22 from December to 12. January.

Rune UR - - - - - - 13 from January to 3. February.

Rune mandrel- - - - - 4 February at 25. February.

Rune OS - - - - - 26 February at 20. March.

Rune RIT - - - - - 21 March-12. April. Rune ka - - - - - 13 from April to 5. can.

Rune HAGAL - - - - - 6 they may be 28. Can.

Rune No - - - - - 29 they may be 20. June. Rune is - - - - - 21 from June to 14. July.

Rune AR - - - - - 15 July-7. August,

Rune SIG - - - - - 8 from August to 30. August. Rune TYR - - - - - 31 August at 22. September. Rune Bar- - - - - 23 September to 15. October. RUNE LAF - - - - - 16 October-7. November.

Rune MAN - - - - - 8 November-29. November,

Rune YR - - - - - 30 from November to 21. December.

Rune hein - - - - - symbolizes the wedding of the whole year. Rune GIBOR symbolizes life-death and rebirth for the New Year.

Do not forget to perform a powerful rune magic; you need the right

colors, good runes, and the right time.

Chapter 19

Viking Rune Casting Tips and Information

These runes work on a deep spiritual level with the subconscious, and it is important to remember that casting Runes is not a prediction of the future. The whole universe is reflected symbols of the rune, so when you ask a question, all spiritual effects are focused on the runes, and therefore, the chosen rune is not accidental, but the choice made by your subconscious.

Used by the Vikings who understood the idea of cause and effect and knew that all things are connected, Rune casting is a type of divination, which is based on an ancient form of psychology. A psychic focus on a single problem when reading with Rune stones to give a thorough check of past, present, and future. What is happening now, and the direction, the future is always seen as changeable, so there is an opportunity to look at the past.

Although people who do not know the process believe it deals with mystery, casting rune is neither supernatural nor mysterious. Casting Runes is not considered an empire of witchcraft, magic, or anything that would tell you happiness.

What Rune casting does is to examine the person and path you are in life, and may try to predict the outcome, if the person stays on this road.

Dowsing or divination by pendulum or bent stick is a similar thing and can be seen as a manifestation of the subconscious, and not a supernatural act. Make sure it's a Quiet Place as you don't want to be disturbed, so that you have to find a suitable place to cast rune stones. You should already have boundaries written on the cloth, and is also useful if you can face north, so place your Rune cloth in front of you on a hard surface. If you have the runes, throw and read it, it is important to the question you want to ask, and when the runes are thrown and read, keep this question in mind when reading.

All runes should have the same shape or size, so they are not recognized from each other, and once decided on it, gently mix the rune stones in the cover until you feel the desire, then pick from the envelope.

Until you have the right number of layouts to use, mix rune stones, and drawing from a bag, this is called Rune casting.

Because each rune can have multiple meanings, it is for the reader to determine which meaning applies to the question, so using your intuition while reading the runes. The cast of Nora involves drawing three runes, one by one, from the bag of runes, they are then laid out in a row, when it comes to casting the runes, there are several ways to cast, for example. The third has to do with the future, and the result is the situation. If you follow the path to the present, and the first rune represents the past situation, the second is the present and represents the location where the person is located.

Vikings Used Rune Songs for Healing

The attitude I took was about 21th Century Rune Master, Port rune to 21th Century, use and do not return to the Viking age (mentally or emotionally.)

Go back in time, using magic, running, energy, they are full of dangers and usually contain unwanted luggage lost.

But we still need to understand the past so that we can use it and not make the same mistakes in the present.

Many of the runes used by our ancestors were grouped into nine songs. Four were devoted to health and safety. For prevention, they can not do this. The remaining five Rune Songs are for victory, magic, word, and spirit.

Many secret medical races are contained in the ancient Scandinavian, Icelandic and Irish sagas, Celtic and Germanic legends, and ancient English fear Beowulf. I'll touch them.

Rune healing miracles, as found in the Icelandic saga grumpy Killer, tells the story of a woman whose close relative was killed.

He took the corpse and gently put it in a wheelchair, then took it home, cleaned and bandaged his wounds, marked them with runes. When he stopped, he started talking.

Remember the movie "Conan" when the witch painted the runes on Conan's corpse? He came to life.

In the saga of men, vapnfjord talks about a doctor or healer named Thorvard. He was considered the best healer of the camp.

He spent seven nights treating the severely injured Thorkel, using his Russian skills. Thorkell was cared for, and Thorvard was given a horse and a silver bracelet. What a reward.

In the saga of Gretta, Gretta is injured, and gangrene began to appear. His brother Illugel treated him with runes. He followed him day and night, taking care of nothing else. Gretta's healed.

Runic healing also takes place in the saga of King H Rolf. King Hrolf suffered two wounds to his hands and lost an eye. Queen yrea cured him.

In the history of Egil and Asmund, we learn about Operation Viking.

Egil lost an arm in battle, and the Dwarf made a stump. Dwarf Egil made a sword, which had a handle in the form of a handle so that he could use it.

Egil then met the old giant, who held his hand and wrapped in herbs."He was waiting for Egil to put his hand on his hand," he said.

"Pulled out the drawer, numb emanate, and cut the stump." He gave there was life, wrapped in silk, and sang his rune song.

Three days later, Egil took full advantage of his hand and eye.

Our ancestors had impressive medical knowledge to help runes and herbs.

I don't put runes in my book so that everyone can see them. Magic in healing competitions is the price paid by the researcher. The price for drinking, perseverance, and willingness to look for themselves. Donations have no value. If hidden, the price is not paid.

Chapter 20

Building the Rune Sorcery Ritual

All the great magicians used their spirits. Their power was in their minds. The runes of magicians are no different.

If you remember the Disney film "The Apprentice of assistants," you will see the workshop. It is full of all kinds of spells, elixirs, potions, and books.

But in the final accounting, he was and is the "spirit" of a magician who has the power to do magic.

Every magical instrument, potion, comes out in his lab was deeply rooted in his mind. He just had to conjure up in his mind what he wanted, and then send it mentally.

But like all disciples in any art, rune magic is art; you must use and learn the physical tools of your workshop.

Once you master them and use them physically, for a while, they will begin to be integrated into your mind.

Now close your eyes and do what you can!

Becoming powerful is a slow, constant, and cumulative process. It will take patience and dedication. If you are in a hurry for a quick result, it is better for this article, starting from.

Primary keys are runes. You must have runes in you.

Runes are universal creative energy. They are the key to the power of the universe. They exist in the quantum ocean as an individual, divine, projects, or energy packages.

With meditation, breathing exercises, and yoga, you can extract these energies from the quantum ocean and fill your aura with them.

Whatever energy you carry in your aura, you can use it. You can use your mind to project these powerful energies anywhere, any distance.

You can use them to attract health, wealth, and love or whatever you want for yourself and your loved ones. You can do everything with your mind.

Be patient, as I add these instructions and articles to the network. Slow and far!

Let's talk; when you practice your witchcraft rituals, you include cleaner energy.

You need to know everything about the runes. Start navigating and studying the runes.

Take a large notebook and start taking notes. One hour a day of study and training will soon see you on your way to becoming a powerful racing magician.

It is ridiculous to believe that you can buy a rune book online, read the rune spell, and wait for results.

The power of all the works of the runes is contained in the wizard. The power is not in the book, a spell, or an instrument, that is, a wand, etc.

To send Runic energy, you must have Runic energy in you. Start Now! On the first page of your large notebook, please insert the date and write in red ink (it symbolizes your blood.)

"I am a powerful racing magician!" Sign it, and start it.

www.ingramcontent.com/pod-product-compliance
Lightning Source LLC
Chambersburg PA
CBHW071500080526
44587CB00014B/2160